正 15 收

Daring
DALMATIANS

ENERGETIC! PROTECTIVE! PLAYFUL!

OBEDIENT! SENSITIVE! LOYAL!

ABDO
Publishing Company

Pam Scheunemann

Consulting Editor, Diane Craig, M.A./Reading Specialist

Published by ABDO Publishing Company
8000 West 78th Street, Edina, Minnesota 55439.

Printed in the United States of America,
North Mankato, Minnesota
052010
092010

 PRINTED ON RECYCLED PAPER

Editor: Liz Salzmann
Content Developer: Nancy Tuminelly
Cover and Interior Design and Production:
   Anders Hanson, Mighty Media
Illustrations: Bob Doucet
Photo Credits: Shutterstock

Library of Congress Cataloging-in-Publication Data
Scheunemann, Pam, 1955-
  Daring dalmatians / by Pam Scheunemann ; illustrated by
Bob Doucet.
    p. cm. -- (Dog daze)
  ISBN 978-1-61613-378-8
  1. Dalmatian dog--Juvenile literature. I. Doucet, Bob, ill. II.
Title.
  SF429.D3S37 2010
  636.72--dc22

                    2010001575

CONTENTS

The
DALMATIAN

The Dalmatian was **bred** to run. It needs to have space for running and jumping. It is the only breed of dog that has spots.

Dalmatians love to be with people and can be good guard dogs. Dalmatians need a lot of attention.

FACIAL FEATURES

Head

The Dalmatian's head is flat on top. The cheeks blend into the strong, narrow **muzzle**.

Teeth and Mouth

The Dalmatian's lower teeth fit just behind the upper teeth.

Eyes

Dalmatians have brown or blue eyes.

Ears

The ears of the Dalmatian are medium sized. They hang close to the head.

4

BODY BASICS

Size

Dalmatians weigh 40 to 60 pounds (18 to 27 kg). They are 19 to 23 inches (48 to 58 cm) tall.

Build

The Dalmatian has a strong, sturdy body. Its back is straight and level.

Tail

The tail of the Dalmatian is thick at the base. It is thinner at the tip.

Legs and Feet

The front legs of the Dalmatian are very straight. Their feet are round and have thick pads.

COAT & COLOR

WHITE FUR

BLACK FUR

LIVER FUR

Dalmatian Fur

The Dalmatian has a short, **dense** coat. It is smooth and looks sleek and shiny.

Dalmatians are white with dark spots. The spots are usually round. Some Dalmatians have spots that overlap and form color masses. Each Dalmatian has a different pattern of spots.

Dalmatian puppies are white when they are born. The spots start appearing when they are about two weeks old.

A Dalmatian's spots are usually black or liver-colored.

BLACK-SPOTTED COAT

LIVER-SPOTTED COAT

HEALTH & CARE

Life Span

Most Dalmatians live about 11 to 14 years.

Grooming

Dalmatians **shed** all year long. It's a good idea to brush Dalmatians often. That helps keep most of the fur from getting on clothes and furniture. Most Dalmatians don't need baths unless they get really dirty.

VET'S CHECKLIST

- Have your Dalmatian spayed or neutered. This will prevent unwanted puppies.

- Visit a vet for regular checkups.

- Ask your vet about which foods are right for your Dalmatian.

- Do not let your Dalmatian overeat.

- Clean your Dalmatian's teeth at least twice a week.

- Make sure your Dalmatian gets a lot of exercise.

EXERCISE & TRAINING

Activity Level

Dalmatians are very active dogs. They need exercise every day. They enjoy running and playing. They should have toys so they don't get bored.

Obedience

Dalmatians are smart and eager to please. But they need **consistent**, firm training. Dalmatians should be socialized when they are young. This means they should meet a lot of people and dogs. Otherwise, they might be **aggressive** toward strangers.

A Few Things You'll Need

A **leash** lets your Dalmatian know that you are the boss. With a leash, you can guide your dog where you want it to go. Most cities require that dogs be on leashes when they are outside.

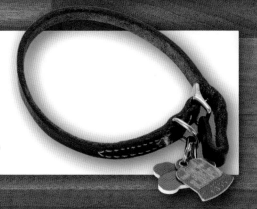

A **collar** is a strap that goes around your Dalmatian's neck. You can attach a leash to the collar to take your dog on walks. You should also attach an **identification tag** with your home address. If your dog ever gets lost, people will know where it lives.

Toys keep your dog healthy and happy. Dogs like to chase and chew on them.

A **dog bed** will help your pet feel safe and comfortable at night.

ATTITUDE & INTELLIGENCE

Personality

Dalmatians love to be around people. They usually get along with other pets after they get used to them. Dalmatians may be too **energetic** for young children or babies.

Intellect

Dalmatians are very intelligent dogs. They can learn new things quickly. They learn best when given treats and praise for doing well. With the right training, Dalmatians can be good watchdogs.

All About Me

Hi! My name is Dottie. I'm a Dalmatian. I just wanted to let you know a few things about me. I made some lists below of things I like and dislike. Check them out!

Things I Like

- Getting a lot of exercise
- Showing my excitement
- Running
- Swimming
- Being with my family

Things I Dislike

- Being ignored
- Being left alone
- Getting bored
- Not getting enough exercise
- Being left outside when it's cold

LITTERS & PUPPIES

Litter Size

Female Dalmatians usually give birth to six to eight puppies.

Diet

Newborn pups drink their mother's milk. Dalmatians can begin to eat soft puppy food when they are about three to four weeks old.

Growth

Puppies should stay with their mothers until they are about eight weeks old. They reach their adult size in 12 to 18 months.

BUYING A DALMATIAN

Choosing a Breeder

It's best to buy a puppy from a **breeder**, not a pet store. When you visit a dog breeder, ask to see the mother and father of the puppies. Make sure the parents are healthy, friendly, and well behaved.

Picking a Puppy

Choose a puppy that isn't too **aggressive** or too shy. If you crouch down, some of the puppies may want to play with you. One of them might be the right one for you!

Is It the Right Dog for You?

Buying a dog is a big decision. You'll want to make sure your new pet suits your lifestyle.

Get out a piece of paper. Draw a line down the middle.

Read the statements listed here. Each time you agree with a statement from the left column, make a mark on the left side of your paper. When you agree with a statement from the right column, make a mark on the right side of your paper.

I like to play with my dog.	☐	☐	I want my dog to entertain itself.
I want to work on training my dog.	☐	☐	I don't care if my dog is trained.
I am home often.	☐	☐	I am not home very often.
I like to bring my pet wherever I go.	☐	☐	I prefer to leave my dog at home.
I have a fenced-in yard.	☐	☐	I live in an apartment.
I enjoy brushing my dog.	☐	☐	I don't like to have to brush my dog.

If you marked more X's on the left side than on the right side, a Dalmatian may be the right dog for you! If you have more X's on the right side of your paper, you might want to consider another breed.

THE COACH DOG

The Dalmatian has been a working dog **breed** for hundreds of years. They have been trained as hunting dogs, guard dogs, rat catchers, circus dogs, shepherd dogs, and coaching dogs.

Dalmatians became known as coaching dogs in England in the 1800s. Since they could run long distances, they were the perfect road dogs. Dalmatians were trained to run alongside coaches, or even under the **axles**!

On crowded streets, the Dalmatian could help clear the way for the coach. When the coach stopped, the Dalmatian guarded the horses and the coach.

Tails of Lore
THE FIREHOUSE DOG

Dalmatians
continued
their role as
coaching dogs
in early firehouses. They would run with the
horses to the fire. Then they would stand and
guard the fire engine. Of course, firefighters
don't use horses and wagons anymore. But many
firehouses today have a Dalmatian as a **mascot**.

One special firehouse dog is a Dalmatian named Wilshire. He was adopted by the Los Angeles Fire Department's Fire Station 29. Now Wilshire is part of the crew. He works out on a treadmill with the firefighters. And he helps save lives by showing kids how to escape a fire. He even has his own Web site!

FIND THE
DALMATIAN

A

B

C

D

THE DALMATIAN QUIZ

1. Dalmatians are not good guard dogs. **True or false?**

2. Dalmatians have green eyes. **True or false?**

3. Dalmatian puppies are white when they are born. **True or false?**

4. Dalmatians enjoy running and playing. **True or false?**

5. Dalmatians can learn new things quickly. **True or false?**

6. Dalmatians were trained to run alongside coaches in England. **True or false?**

Answers: 1) false 2) false 3) true 4) true 5) true 6) true

GLOSSARY

aggressive - likely to attack or confront.

axle - a bar that connects two wheels.

breed - 1. to raise animals that have certain traits. A *breeder* is someone whose job is to breed certain animals. 2. a group of animals with common ancestors.

consistent - always done the same way.

dense - thick or crowded together.

energetic - active and full of energy.

mascot - a person, animal, or object that is supposed to bring good luck to a team or an organization.

muzzle - an animal's nose and jaws.

obedience - doing what one is told to do.

shed - to lose something, such as skin, leaves, or fur, through a natural process.

About SUPER SANDCASTLE™

Bigger Books for Emerging Readers
Grades K–4

Created for library, classroom, and at-home use, Super SandCastle™ books support and engage young readers as they develop and build literacy skills and will increase their general knowledge about the world around them. Super SandCastle™ books are part of SandCastle,™ the leading preK–3 imprint for emerging and beginning readers. Super SandCastle™ features a larger trim size for more reading fun.

Let Us Know

Super SandCastle™ would like to hear your stories about reading this book. What was your favorite page? Was there something hard that you needed help with? Share the ups and downs of learning to read. We want to hear from you! Send us an e-mail.

sandcastle@abdopublishing.com

Contact us for a complete list of SandCastle,™ Super SandCastle,™ and other nonfiction and fiction titles from ABDO Publishing Company.

www.abdopublishing.com • 8000 West 78th Street Edina, MN 55439 • 800-800-1312 • 952-831-1632 fax